Explore
Santorini

A Comprehensive 2023 Travel Guide Book

Clifford M. Davis

All rights reserved. No part of this publication may be reproduced, distributed, or transmitted in any form or by any means, including photocopying, recording, or other electronic or mechanical methods, without the prior written permission of the publisher, except in the case of brief quotations embodied in critical reviews and certain other noncommercial uses permitted by copyright law.

Copyright © Clifford M. Davis, 2023.

Table of Content

INTRODUCTION

A Brief History of Santorini

Geography and Climate

Planning Your Trip to Santorini

Getting Around Santorini

Transportation Options

Maps and Itinerary Planning

Accommodations
- Types of Accommodations

Recommendations for Different Budgets

Insider Tips for Booking Accommodations

Exploring the Island
- Popular Attractions

Hidden Gems

Suggested Itineraries for Different Interests

Food and Drink

- Traditional Cuisine of Santorini
- Local Wine and Drinks

Best Restaurants and Tavernas

Beaches and Outdoor Activities
- Types of Beaches
  - Recommended Beaches and Activities

Water Sports and Excursions

Nightlife and Shopping
- Bars, Clubs, and Nightlife

Shopping in Santorini
- Local Products and Souvenirs

CONCLUSION

INTRODUCTION

Santorini, a small island in the Aegean Sea, is one of the most popular tourist destinations in the world. With its unique blend of natural beauty, history, and culture, it is not surprising that people flock here year after year to experience the magic of this place.

Whether you are a first-time visitor or a seasoned traveler, this guidebook will provide you with all the information you need to make the most of your trip to Santorini.

The island of Santorini is located in the southern Aegean Sea and is part of the Cyclades island group. It is famous for its breathtaking views of the Aegean Sea, its crystal-clear waters, and its sunny weather.

The island's most distinctive feature is its volcanic landscape, which includes black and red beaches, towering cliffs, and fascinating volcanic formations. The island's history is also rich and varied, with evidence of human habitation going back thousands of years. Today, Santorini is a thriving tourist destination, known for its sophisticated nightlife, vibrant cultural scene, and breathtaking scenery.

In this guidebook, we will take you on a tour of the island, highlighting its many attractions and sights. We will introduce you to the unique history and culture of Santorini, including its ancient ruins, traditional villages, and local cuisine.

We will also provide practical information, such as how to get around the island, where to stay, and what to see and do. Whether you are interested in history, or culture, or just soaking up the sun and enjoying the stunning views, this guidebook will help you make the most of your trip to Santorini.

So pack your bags, grab your sunscreen, and get ready for an unforgettable adventure on the stunning island of Santorini. Whether you are traveling alone or with family and friends, this guidebook will be your ultimate companion on your journey to this amazing destination.

A Brief History of Santorini

Santorini is a small island located in the Aegean Sea and is part of the Cyclades group of islands in Greece. The island has a rich and fascinating history that spans thousands of years.

The earliest known settlement on Santorini dates back to the 3rd millennium BC, and it was later ruled by the Minoans, an ancient civilization known for their advanced culture and architectural achievements.

The island was a thriving hub of trade and commerce during this time, and its capital, Akrotiri, was considered one of the most important cities in the Aegean.

However, the island's prosperity came to an end in the late 17th century BC when a massive volcanic eruption devastated the island and caused a tsunami that destroyed much of the Minoan civilization. The island lay uninhabited for several centuries until it was rediscovered and resettled by the Dorians in the 9th century BC.

In the classical period, Santorini was a member of the Delian League, an alliance of Greek city-states, and was a prosperous center of trade and commerce. The island was conquered by the Romans in the 1st century BC, and it remained under their rule until the Byzantine period.

In the 13th century, Santorini was ruled by the Venetians, and the island prospered as a center of trade and commerce. During the Ottoman Empire, the island was used as a naval base, and it played an important role in the Greek War of Independence in the 19th century.

Today, Santorini is a popular tourist destination, known for its stunning caldera, picturesque villages, and stunning sunsets. The island's rich history can be seen in its many archaeological sites, including the ancient city of Akrotiri and the medieval castle of Skaros.

Visitors to Santorini can also enjoy its beautiful beaches, traditional villages, and delicious cuisine, making it a must-visit destination for travelers to Greece.

The island of Santorini is famous for its breathtaking views, crystal-clear waters, and stunning sunsets. The caldera, which was formed by a volcanic eruption thousands of years ago, is the main attraction on the island, and visitors can enjoy stunning views of the caldera from various points on the island, including the village of Oia, which is widely considered to be one of the most beautiful villages in Greece.

Santorini is also known for its rich cultural heritage and traditional architecture. The island is dotted with charming villages that have been built in the traditional Cycladic style, with white-washed buildings and blue-domed churches.

The villages of Fira and Oia are particularly popular with visitors and are home to numerous museums, churches, and other cultural attractions.

The island is also famous for its delicious cuisine, which is influenced by the Aegean and Mediterranean regions. Visitors can enjoy traditional dishes such as moussaka, stuffed vine leaves, and fresh seafood, along with local specialties such as tomato keftedes and Santorinian tomatoes.

In recent years, Santorini has become a popular wedding destination, and many couples choose to exchange their vows on the island's stunning beaches or atop its towering cliffs. The island also attracts a large number of tourists each year, who come to enjoy its beautiful scenery, rich history, and vibrant nightlife.

Santorini is also home to several important archaeological sites, including the ancient city of Akrotiri, which was buried by a volcanic eruption in the 17th century BC. The site was rediscovered in the 20th century and has been excavated to reveal a wealth of information about the Minoan civilization. The island also has several ancient ruins, including the medieval castle of Skaros, which dates back to the Venetian period.

Geography and Climate

Santorini is a volcanic island located in the Aegean Sea, part of the Cyclades islands in Greece. It is approximately 120 km southeast of Greece's mainland. Santorini has a unique and striking geography due to its volcanic origins, characterized by its high cliffs, black sand beaches, and the caldera, which is a large crater created by a volcanic eruption.

The island has a Mediterranean climate, with hot, dry summers and mild, wet winters. During the summer, temperatures can reach up to 30°C and occasionally higher, while in the winter, temperatures are usually between 10-15°C.

Despite the dry summer months, Santorini receives occasional rain showers, and the island is also known for its strong winds, particularly the "Meltemi," which is a north wind that blows in the Aegean during the summer.

The volcanic soil of Santorini is rich in minerals, making it suitable for growing grapes, which are used to produce the island's famous Vinsanto wine. The unique topography of the island, combined with its climate, provides ideal conditions for agriculture, allowing for the cultivation of a variety of crops including vineyards, tomatoes, and other fruits and vegetables.

Geography:
- Santorini is the largest island of a small archipelago that also includes the smaller islands of Thirassia, Aspronisi, Palia, and Nea Kameni.

- The island is shaped like a crescent moon, with the caldera-forming the center of the island and the high cliffs surrounding it.

- The cliffs on the island are some of the highest in the world and offer stunning views of the Aegean Sea and the nearby islands.

- In addition to the black sand beaches, Santorini also has several red sand beaches, which are a result of the island's volcanic activity.

Climate:
- The climate in Santorini is typically Mediterranean, with warm, dry summers and mild, wet winters.

- The island experiences significant temperature swings between day and night, especially during the summer months.

- The island is also vulnerable to natural disasters such as earthquakes, due to its volcanic origins.

Tourism:

- Santorini is one of the most popular tourist destinations in Greece and is known for its stunning scenery, unique architecture, and rich cultural heritage.

- The island is home to several ancient sites, including the ruins of the Minoan city of Akrotiri, which is considered to be one of the most important archaeological sites in Greece.

- In addition to its historical sites, Santorini is also famous for its picturesque villages, such as Oia, Fira, and Imerovigli, which are known for their charming architecture and stunning views.

- The island is a popular wedding and honeymoon destination and is also known for its romantic atmosphere.

Planning Your Trip to Santorini

Santorini is a stunningly beautiful and popular tourist destination, and planning your trip to this Greek island can be both exciting and overwhelming. However, with the right planning and preparation, you can ensure that your trip to Santorini is memorable and enjoyable. Here are some tips to help you plan your trip to Santorini:

- **Determine your travel dates**: Santorini is a popular tourist destination, so it is essential to plan your trip well in advance to avoid disappointment. Consider the time of year you plan to travel, as the island can get very busy during the peak tourist season, which typically runs from June to September. If you prefer a more relaxed experience, consider visiting during the shoulder season, which is usually from April to May or October to November.

- **Choose your accommodation**: There is a wide range of accommodation options in Santorini, from budget-friendly apartments to luxurious villas. Consider your budget and the type of experience you're looking for when choosing your accommodation. Some of the most popular areas for accommodation include Oia, Fira, and Imerovigli, which are known for their charming architecture, stunning views, and romantic atmosphere.

- **Plan your transportation**: Santorini is a small island, and there are several transportation options available, including buses, taxis, and rental cars. If you're staying in one of the villages on the island, you may find that you don't need a car, as the villages are connected by a network of bus routes and taxis. However, if you're planning to explore the island more extensively, you may want to consider renting a car.

- **Consider what activities to do**: There is no shortage of things to do in Santorini, from exploring ancient ruins to relaxing on the beach. Some popular activities include visiting the archaeological site of Akrotiri, exploring the villages of Oia, Fira, and Imerovigli, and taking a sunset boat tour of the caldera. Consider what interests you and plan your itinerary accordingly.

- **Make dining reservations**: Santorini is known for its excellent dining scene, and many restaurants can get very busy, especially during the peak tourist season. Consider making dining reservations in advance to ensure that you get to experience the best of Santorini's cuisine.

- **Plan for your budget**: Santorini can be an expensive destination, but with careful planning, you can stay within your budget. Consider the cost of transportation, accommodation, dining, and activities when planning your trip.

- **Pack appropriately**: The climate in Santorini can be quite warm during the summer, so be sure to pack light, comfortable clothing and appropriate footwear for walking and exploring. Don't forget to include sunscreen, sunglasses, and a hat for sun protection.

Getting Around Santorini

Arrival and Departure

Arrival:
- **By plane**: The main airport in Santorini is the Santorini National Airport (JTR), which is located about 5 kilometers southeast of the capital, Thira. The airport has several daily flights to and from Athens and other Greek islands. From the airport, you can take a taxi, bus, or rental car to your accommodation.

- **By ferry**: If you're coming from another Greek island, you can take a ferry to Santorini. The ferry port is located in the village of Athinios, which is about 10 kilometers from Thira. From the ferry port, you can take a taxi, bus, or rental car to your accommodation.

Departure:
- **By plane**: When departing from Santorini, you can take a flight from the Santorini National Airport (JTR) to your next destination. Be sure to arrive at the airport well in advance of your flight, as there may be security checks and check-in procedures to complete.

- **By ferry**: If you're departing from Santorini to another Greek island, you can take a ferry from the ferry port in Athinios. Be sure to arrive at the ferry port well in advance of your departure time, as there may be boarding procedures to complete.

Regardless of your mode of arrival and departure, it's important to plan and allow plenty of time to reach your destination. If you have any questions or concerns about arrival and departure procedures, be sure to check with your airline or ferry company for more information.

- **Check your visa requirements**: If you're not a citizen of the European Union, be sure to check the visa requirements for entering Greece and the EU. You may need to obtain a tourist visa or a Schengen visa, depending on the length of your stay and your nationality.

- **Book your transportation in advance**: Booking your transportation in advance, whether it be a taxi, bus, or rental car, can save you time and hassle upon arrival. This is especially important during peak tourist season when transportation can be limited and in high demand.

- **Pack a carry-on bag**: When traveling by plane or ferry, it's always a good idea to pack a carry-on bag with essentials such as medication, important documents, and a change of clothes in case your luggage is delayed or lost.

- **Check your flight or ferry schedule**: Be sure to check your flight or ferry schedule in advance and allow plenty of time for any unexpected delays. If your flight or ferry is delayed or canceled, be sure to contact your airline or ferry company as soon as possible to make alternative arrangements.

- **Take out travel insurance**: Travel insurance can provide peace of mind in case of unexpected events such as trip cancellations, medical emergencies, or lost luggage. Make sure to research and compare different travel insurance options to find the best coverage for your needs.

Transportation Options

From buses to taxis to rental cars, there are plenty of ways to get around the island and see all that it has to offer.

- **Buses**: The local bus system in Santorini is an affordable and convenient way to get around the island. Multiple bus routes run between the main towns and beaches, making it easy to get from one place to another. The buses are air-conditioned and run frequently, making them a good option for those who want to take in the sights and sounds of Santorini without having to worry about navigating the roads.

- **Taxis**: Taxis are also readily available on the island, and they offer a more flexible and personalized form of transportation. They can be hailed on the street, at taxi stands, or called in advance. They are a good option for those who are looking for a faster or more direct way to get around the island, or for those who prefer not to take public transportation. However, it is important to note that taxis in Santorini can be more expensive than buses or rental cars.

- **Rental Cars**: Renting a car in Santorini is a great way to explore the island at your own pace. This option gives you the freedom to see the sights you want to see and to make stops along the way without having to worry about schedules or wait times. Driving in Santorini can be challenging due to the narrow and winding roads, so it is important to be confident and comfortable behind the wheel before embarking on a road trip.

- **Mopeds and Scooters:** Another popular mode of transportation in Santorini is mopeds and scooters. This option is perfect for those who want a more adventurous and scenic way to explore the island. However, it is important to note that driving a moped or scooter in Santorini can be dangerous due to the roads, so it is important to have experience and be comfortable riding these types of vehicles.

- **Sailing and Boat Tours:** Another unique and exciting way to explore Santorini is by boat. There are many different types of boat tours available, from sunset cruises to snorkeling excursions to island hopping tours. This is a great way to see the island from a different perspective and to get a glimpse of the beautiful Aegean Sea. The boat tours usually depart from the main port of Athinios, and they provide a great opportunity to relax and enjoy the scenery while getting a taste of the local culture and traditions.

- **Donkeys and Horses**: For those who want to experience Santorini in a more traditional way, donkey and horse rides are available in certain areas of the island. This is a fun and unique way to see the island, and it provides a more intimate and personal connection with the local environment.

Maps and Itinerary Planning

If you're planning a trip to Santorini, a good map and itinerary are essential to make the most of your time on the island.

One of the first things to do when planning a trip to Santorini is to get a good map of the island. There are many options available online, including Google Maps, which can be accessed on your smartphone or tablet. These maps will help you get a sense of the different areas of the island and the locations of the major tourist attractions.

When planning your itinerary, it's important to consider the time of year you're visiting Santorini. The island is busiest in the summer months, from June to August when temperatures can be quite hot. If you're visiting during the off-season, from September to May, you'll find that the island is less crowded and you'll have more time to explore at your own pace.

One of the top tourist attractions in Santorini is the town of Oia, which is known for its stunning sunsets. To make the most of your time in Oia, it's recommended that you arrive in the late afternoon and spend some time exploring the town and taking in the views before settling in to watch the sunset. After the sun sets, you can enjoy a leisurely dinner at one of the many restaurants in Oia.

Another must-see attraction in Santorini is the ancient city of Akrotiri. This is one of the most important archaeological sites in Greece and provides a fascinating glimpse into the island's rich history. Visitors can explore the ruins of the city and learn about the way of life of the people who lived there thousands of years ago.

For those who want to relax and soak up the sun, there are many beautiful beaches in Santorini to choose from. Red Beach, Perissa, and Kamari are a few of the most well-known beaches. Whether you prefer to lounge on the sand or go for a swim, you're sure to find a beach that suits your needs.

Finally, don't forget to make time for some of the other amazing attractions in Santorini, such as Therma Springs, the Venetian castle in Firá, and the picturesque village of Megalochori. With so much to see and do, it's easy to see why Santorini is one of the most popular tourist destinations in Greece.

Accommodations

Types of Accommodations

- **Hotels**: Santorini is home to a wide range of hotels, ranging from budget-friendly options to luxurious five-star establishments. Many of the hotels in Santorini are located in the towns of Fira, Oia, and Imerovigli, which offer stunning views of the Aegean Sea and the caldera. If you're looking for a hotel with a pool and easy access to the beach, consider staying in Perissa or Kamari.

- **Villas**: For those who prefer more privacy and space, villas in Santorini can be a great option. These properties often come with a private pool, kitchen, and outdoor living area, making them a popular choice for families and groups of friends. Villas in Santorini can be found in a variety of locations, including Oia, Imerovigli, and Perissa.

- **Boutique Hotels**: For a more intimate and personalized experience, consider staying at one of Santorini's boutique hotels. These small hotels offer unique and stylish accommodations, often with traditional Greek design elements. Many boutique hotels in Santorini are located in the charming villages of Oia and Imerovigli and offer breathtaking views of the Aegean Sea.

- **Cave Houses**: For a truly authentic Santorinian experience, consider staying in a cave house. These homes, which are carved into the cliffside, offer a unique and atmospheric way to experience the island. Many cave houses in Santorini come with their private terrace and pool and offer stunning views of the sea and the caldera.

- **Bed and Breakfasts**: For those who want a more personal touch, a bed, and breakfast in Santorini can be a great option. These properties are often run by local families and offer a warm and welcoming atmosphere. Bed and breakfasts in Santorini can be found in a variety of locations, including Fira, Oia, and Imerovigli.

- **Apartments**: For those who prefer self-catering accommodations, apartments in Santorini can be a convenient and affordable option. These properties come with their kitchen and living areas, allowing you to enjoy meals at your leisure. Apartments in Santorini can be found in many of the towns and villages on the island, including Fira, Oia, and Perissa.

- **Luxury Resorts**: For those looking for the ultimate in luxury, Santorini has several world-class resorts. These properties often feature elegant rooms, top-notch amenities, and stunning views of the Aegean Sea. Many luxury resorts in Santorini are located in secluded locations, offering peace and tranquility away from the hustle and bustle of the island's towns and villages.

- **Traditional Houses**: For a true immersion in Santorinian culture, consider staying in a traditional house. These homes, often made from stone and featuring traditional Greek architecture, offer a unique and authentic experience of the island. Many traditional houses in Santorini come with private courtyards and terraces and are often located in the charming villages of Oia and Imerovigli.

- **Studios**: For a simple and budget-friendly option, consider staying in a studio in Santorini. These properties typically feature a small kitchenette and sleeping area, making them a great choice for solo travelers or couples. Studios in Santorini can be found in many of the towns and villages on the island, including Fira, Oia, and Perissa.

- **Yachts**: For those looking for a unique and adventurous experience, consider renting a yacht in Santorini. This option allows you to explore the Aegean Sea and visit the other Greek islands in style and comfort. Many companies offer yacht rentals in Santorini, and many include a captain and crew to take care of all the details.

Recommendations for Different Budgets

Budget:

- **Studios**: Studios in Santorini offer a budget-friendly option for solo travelers or couples. These properties typically feature a small kitchenette and sleeping area and are often located in the towns of Fira, Oia, and Perissa.

- **Hostels**: For the budget-conscious traveler, several hostels in Santorini offer affordable dormitory-style rooms.

- **Traditional Houses**: For a unique and authentic experience, consider staying in a traditional house in Santorini. Many of these homes are located in the charming villages of Oia and Imerovigli and offer a budget-friendly alternative to more expensive accommodations.

Mid-Range:

- **Hotels**: Many hotels in Santorini offer comfortable and affordable accommodations. Many of these hotels are located in the towns of Fira, Oia, and Imerovigli and offer stunning views of the Aegean Sea.

- **Bed and Breakfasts**: For a more personal touch, consider staying at a bed and breakfast in Santorini. These properties are often run by local families and offer a warm and welcoming atmosphere.

- **Apartments**: For those who prefer self-catering accommodations, apartments in Santorini can be a convenient and affordable option. These properties come with their kitchen and living area and can be found in many of the towns and villages on the island.

Luxury:

- **Villas**: For those looking for privacy and luxury, villas in Santorini offer a great option. These properties often come with their private pool, kitchen, and outdoor living area, and can be found in a variety of locations, including Oia, Imerovigli, and Perissa.

- **Luxury Resorts**: For the ultimate in luxury, several world-class resorts in Santorini offer elegant rooms, top-notch amenities, and stunning views of the Aegean Sea.

- **Cave Houses**: For a truly unique and luxurious experience, consider staying in a cave house in Santorini. These homes, which are carved into the cliffside, offer a one-of-a-kind experience and often come with a private terrace and pool.

Insider Tips for Booking Accommodations

- **Plan ahead**: Santorini is a popular tourist destination and it can be difficult to find available accommodations during peak season (July and August). Book well in advance to ensure that you have a place to stay during your trip.

- **Choose the right location**: Santorini has several villages, each with its unique character. Decide on the type of experience you want (beach or caldera view, traditional or modern, etc.) and choose your accommodation accordingly.

- **Consider alternative accommodation options**: In addition to traditional hotels and resorts, Santorini also offers a range of alternative accommodations, such as villas, apartments, and caves. These options can provide a more unique and authentic experience.

- **Read reviews**: Before booking your accommodation, take the time to read reviews from other travelers. This can give you a better idea of the facilities, services, and overall experience you can expect.

- **Negotiate rates**: If you're traveling during the low season, it may be possible to negotiate lower rates with hotels and resorts. Never hesitate to request a price reduction!

- **Book directly**: Booking directly with the hotel or resort can often result in better rates and more flexibility with your reservation.

- **Check for added services**: Many accommodations in Santorini offer added services, such as airport transfers, rental cars, and tours. These can save you money and make your trip more convenient.

- **Consider the size of your party**: If you're traveling with a large group, consider booking a villa or multiple rooms at a hotel. This can be a more cost-effective option than booking separate rooms at different accommodations.

- **Check for seasonal promotions**: Many accommodations offer seasonal promotions and discounts, so be sure to check for any available deals before making your booking.

- **Be flexible**: If you're traveling during the high season, consider being flexible with your travel dates. Booking a room a few days before or after your preferred dates may result in lower rates and better availability.

Exploring the Island

Popular Attractions

- **Oia**: This is a charming village located in the northwestern part of the island and is known for its traditional architecture and breathtaking views. Visitors can walk through the narrow streets and admire the beautiful blue-domed churches, whitewashed houses, and scenic vistas. Oia is also famous for its sunset views, where visitors can watch the sun dip below the horizon over the Aegean Sea.

- **Fira**: This is the capital of Santorini and is known for its traditional architecture, narrow streets, and stunning views. Visitors can walk along the cobblestone streets and admire the beautiful churches, traditional houses, and stunning views of the Aegean Sea. Fira is also famous for its nightlife, with many bars, restaurants, and clubs that are open until the early hours of the morning.

- **Akrotiri Archaeological Site**: This is an ancient Minoan settlement that was preserved by the volcanic ash that covered it after the volcanic eruption in the 16th century BC. Visitors can see well-preserved buildings, frescoes, and artifacts from this ancient civilization. The site offers a glimpse into the past and is a must-visit for history enthusiasts.

- **Santorini Black Beach**: This is a beautiful beach located in the southern part of the island and is known for its black sand, crystal-clear waters, and stunning views. Visitors can enjoy a variety of water sports, relax on the sand, or take a dip in the sea. The beach is surrounded by cafes, bars, and restaurants, making it a great place to spend the day.

- **Red Beach**: This is another popular beach located in the southern part of the island and is known for its red sand and rock formations. The red sand is a result of the volcanic activity on the island, and the rock formations provide a stunning backdrop for sunbathing and swimming. In crystal-clear waters, guests can also go diving and snorkeling.

- **Thira**: This is a beautiful village located in the western part of the island and is known for its traditional architecture and stunning views. Visitors can walk through the narrow streets, admire the beautiful churches, and take in the views of the Aegean Sea. Thira is also famous for its sunset views and is a popular spot for watching the sun dip below the horizon.

- **Ancient Thira**: This is an ancient city that was built on the western side of the island and offers breathtaking views of the Aegean Sea. Visitors can see the remains of the ancient city, including the theater, agora, and temples. The site offers a glimpse into the past and is a must-visit for history enthusiasts.

- **Amoudi Bay**: This is a picturesque bay located at the foot of Oia and is known for its crystal-clear waters, stunning views, and traditional tavernas. Visitors can take a swim in the sea, enjoy a meal at one of the tavernas, or go snorkeling and discover the vibrant marine life in the bay.

- **Megalochori Village**: This is a traditional village located in the center of the island and is known for its beautiful churches, historic houses, and peaceful atmosphere. Visitors can stroll through the narrow streets, admire the architecture, and visit one of the many wineries in the area. The village is also a great place to enjoy a meal or drink at one of the local tavernas.

- **Skaros Rock**: This is a large rock formation located in Imerovigli and offers stunning views of the Aegean Sea. Visitors can climb to the top of the rock and enjoy panoramic views of the island and the sea. Skaros Rock is also a popular spot for watching the sunset.

- **Pyrgos Village**: This is a traditional village located in the center of the island and is known for its Venetian architecture, beautiful churches, and peaceful atmosphere. Visitors can stroll through the narrow streets, admire the architecture, and visit one of the many wineries in the area. The village is also a great place to enjoy a meal or drink at one of the local tavernas.

- **Monastery of Prophet Elias**: This is a beautiful monastery located on top of a hill in the center of the island and offers stunning views of the Aegean Sea. Visitors can climb to the top of the hill and admire the architecture of the monastery, as well as the views of the surrounding area. The monastery is also a popular spot for watching the sunset.

- **Therma Beach**: This is a hot springs beach located on the east coast of the island and is known for its therapeutic properties. Visitors can relax in the warm waters, which are rich in minerals and said to have healing properties. The beach is also a great place to go snorkeling and discover the vibrant marine life in the area.

- **Kamari Beach**: This is a long, sandy beach located on the east coast of the island and is known for its crystal-clear waters, beach bars, and water sports. Visitors can relax on the sand, swim in the sea, or participate in a variety of water sports, including parasailing, jet-skiing, and windsurfing. Kamari Beach is also a popular spot for watching the sunset.

- **Vlychada Beach**: This is a stunning beach located on the south coast of the island and is known for its dramatic rock formations, crystal-clear waters, and serene atmosphere. Visitors can relax on the sand, swim in the sea, or go snorkeling and discover the vibrant marine life in the area.

- **Perissa Beach**: This is a long, sandy beach located on the southeast coast of the island and is known for its crystal-clear waters, beach bars, and water sports. Visitors can relax on the sand, swim in the sea, or participate in a variety of water sports, including paddleboarding, kayaking, and windsurfing. Perissa Beach is also a popular spot for watching the sunset.

- **Mesa Gonia Village**: This is a traditional village located on the south coast of the island and is known for its picturesque architecture, beautiful churches, and serene atmosphere. Visitors can stroll through the narrow streets, admire the architecture, and visit one of the many wineries in the area. The village is also a great place to enjoy a meal or drink at one of the local tavernas.

- **Emporio Village**: This is a charming village located on the southeast coast of the island and is known for its traditional architecture, beautiful churches, and scenic vistas. Visitors can walk through the narrow streets, admire the architecture, and take in the views of the Aegean Sea. Emporio Village is also famous for its sunset views and is a popular spot for watching the sun dip below the horizon.

- **Santorini Art Space**: This is a contemporary art center located in Fira and features works by local and international artists. Visitors can explore the galleries, attend exhibitions, and participate in workshops and classes. The center is a great place for art lovers to discover new artists and admire contemporary works.

- **The Santorini Cable Car**: This is a cable car that takes visitors from the port of Athinios to the top of the cliff in Fira, offering breathtaking views of the Aegean Sea and the caldera. The journey takes about 5 minutes and is a popular way for visitors to reach the town of Fira without having to hike up the steep steps.

- **The Red Beach**: This is a unique beach located on the southern coast of the island and is known for its distinctive red sand and striking rock formations. Visitors can relax on the sand, swim in crystal-clear waters, or go snorkeling and discover the vibrant marine life in the area.

- **The Archaeological Museum of Thera**: This is a museum located in Fira that showcases artifacts from the ancient city of Thera, which was buried by the volcanic eruption on the island in the 17th century BC. Visitors can see items such as pottery, jewelry, and sculptures, and learn about the history of the island and its people.

- **The Wine Museum**: This is a museum located in Megalochori that showcases the history and culture of winemaking in Santorini. Visitors can learn about the local winemaking traditions, the different types of grapes grown on the island, and the wine-making process. The museum also has a tasting room where visitors can sample some of the local wines.

- **The Open-Air Cinema**: This is an outdoor cinema located in Kamari that is open in the summer months and shows a variety of films, including classic films and contemporary releases. Visitors can relax under the stars, enjoy a drink, and watch a movie in a unique and memorable setting.

- **The Ancient Thira**: This is an archaeological site located on the southern coast of the island and is the remains of the ancient city of Thira, which was inhabited from the 9th century BC to the 3rd century AD. Visitors can explore the ruins of the city, including the theater, agora, and houses, and learn about the history and culture of the island's ancient people.

Hidden Gems

There are many hidden gems to be found on this beautiful Greek island. Here are some of the most notable hidden gems in Santorini:

- **Ammoudi Bay**: This is a small bay located on the west coast of the island that is known for its clear waters, excellent seafood, and stunning views. Visitors can take a boat tour from Oia and explore the area, swim in the crystal-clear waters, or enjoy a meal at one of the local tavernas.

- **The Black Beach**: This is a black sand beach located on the southeast coast of the island and is known for its unique sand and dramatic rock formations. Visitors can relax on the sand, swim in the sea, or go snorkeling and discover the vibrant marine life in the area.

- **The Venetian Castle**: This is a castle located in the town of Akrotiri and is a well-preserved example of Venetian architecture. Visitors can explore the castle, admire the architecture, and take in the stunning views of the Aegean Sea.

- **The Byzantine Castle**: This is a castle located in the town of Ia and is a well-preserved example of Byzantine architecture. Visitors can explore the castle, admire the architecture, and take in the stunning views of the Aegean Sea.

- **The Aegean Maritime Museum**: This is a museum located in Oia that showcases the maritime history of the Aegean Sea and the island of Santorini. Visitors can learn about the local maritime traditions, the history of shipbuilding, and the traditional fishing practices of the island.

- **The Folklore Museum of Emporio**: This is a museum located in the village of Emporio and showcases the traditional folk art and customs of the island. Visitors can see items such as traditional clothing, jewelry, and pottery, and learn about the history and culture of the island's people.

- **The Geological Museum**: This is a museum located in the town of Megalochori that showcases the geological history of the island and the volcanic eruption that shaped the island's unique landscapes. Visitors can learn about the geological processes that created the island, see samples of volcanic rock and ash, and discover the geological history of the Aegean Sea.

- **The Perissa Beach**: This is a black sand beach located on the southeast coast of the island and is known for its unique sand, clear waters, and relaxed atmosphere. Visitors can relax on the sand, swim in the sea, or try one of the many water sports activities available in the area.

- **The Vlichada Beach**: This is a secluded beach located on the south coast of the island and is known for its stunning natural beauty and crystal-clear waters. Visitors can relax on the sand, swim in the sea, or explore the nearby caves and rock formations.

- **The Finikia Village**: This is a traditional village located in the center of the island and is known for its well-preserved architecture and relaxed atmosphere. Visitors can explore the narrow streets, admire the architecture, and visit the local tavernas and shops.

- **The Ancient Therma**: This is a hot spring located on the southeast coast of the island and is known for its therapeutic properties and stunning views of the Aegean Sea. Visitors can relax in the hot spring, soak up the scenery, and enjoy a soak in the warm waters.

- **The Art Space Gallery**: This is a contemporary art gallery located in the village of Oia and showcases the works of local and international artists. Visitors can admire the art, learn about contemporary art and artists, and purchase unique pieces to take home.

- **The Baxedes Beach**: This is a secluded beach located on the south coast of the island and is known for its stunning natural beauty and clear waters. Visitors can relax on the sand, swim in the sea, or go snorkeling and discover the vibrant marine life in the area.

- **The Santorini Nature Trail:** This is a hiking trail that takes visitors through the island's stunning landscapes and offers panoramic views of the Aegean Sea and the caldera. Visitors can hike through the vineyards, olive groves, and volcanic landscapes, and discover the island's unique flora and fauna.

- **The Museum of Prehistoric Thira:** This is a museum located in the town of Fira that showcases the ancient history of the island and the findings from the excavations of the ancient city of Thira. Visitors can learn about the history and culture of the ancient people of Santorini and see artifacts such as pottery, jewelry, and sculptures.

- **The Megalochori Windmills**: This is a group of windmills located in the village of Megalochori and is a well-preserved example of traditional Aegean architecture. Visitors can admire the windmills, learn about their history and significance, and take in stunning views of the Aegean Sea.

- **The Ilias Lalaounis Jewelry Museum**: This is a museum located in the town of Fira that showcases the works of the Greek jewelry designer Ilias Lalaounis. Visitors can admire the jewelry, learn about the designer and his techniques, and purchase unique pieces to take home.

- **The Santorini Waterfall**: This is a hidden waterfall located in the northern part of the island and is known for its stunning beauty and serene atmosphere. Visitors can hike to the waterfall, swim in the clear waters, and admire the surrounding landscapes.

- **The Red Beach**: This is a red sand beach located on the south coast of the island and is known for its unique sand, clear waters, and dramatic rock formations. Visitors can relax on the sand, swim in the sea, or go snorkeling and discover the vibrant marine life in the area.

- **Saint Nicholas Chapel**: This is a small chapel located in the village of Oia and is known for its traditional Aegean architecture and stunning views of the Aegean Sea. Visitors can admire the chapel, learn about its history and significance, and take in the breathtaking views of the surrounding landscapes.

Suggested Itineraries for Different Interests

History and Culture Enthusiast:
Start your day by visiting the ancient city of Akrotiri, one of the most well-preserved Minoan settlements in the world. This ancient city offers a unique insight into the civilization that once inhabited the island. Next, visit the Museum of Prehistoric Thira, where you can learn about the history of Santorini and the ancient civilization that lived here. In the afternoon, visit the traditional villages of Oia and Fira, where you can see the famous blue-domed churches, traditional buildings, and winding streets. End your day with a visit to the Venetian Castle in Ia, where you can enjoy panoramic views of the island and the Aegean Sea.

Foodie:
Start your day with a visit to the local food market in Fira, where you can sample fresh, local produce and taste some of the delicious traditional dishes of Santorini. Next, visit one of the many vineyards on the island, where you can sample the local wine and learn about the wine-making process. For lunch, head to one of the traditional tavernas in Oia, where you can sample some of the best local cuisine, including grilled fish, fresh salads, and delicious sweets. End your day with a sunset dinner at a restaurant in Ia, where you can enjoy the views of the Aegean Sea as you sample some of the finest cuisines in Santorini.

Beach-Goer:
Start your day with a visit to the famous Red Beach, where you can swim in crystal-clear waters and relax on the sand. Next, visit Black Beach, where you can relax in the shade and soak up the sun. In the afternoon, visit Perissa Beach, where you can enjoy water sports,

including surfing, windsurfing, and kitesurfing. End your day with a visit to Vlychada Beach, where you can watch the sunset and enjoy a relaxing evening by the sea.

Adventure Seeker:
Start your day with a hike to the top of the ancient volcano, where you can enjoy breathtaking views of the island and the Aegean Sea. Next, go scuba diving in the waters around Santorini, where you can explore the vibrant marine life and shipwrecks. In the afternoon, take a boat tour around the island, where you can visit some of the hidden beaches and caves. End your day with a sunset catamaran tour, where you can sail around the island and enjoy the views as the sun sets over the Aegean Sea.

Photography Enthusiast:
Start your day with a visit to the famous Blue Dome churches in Oia, where you can take stunning photos of the iconic blue-domed

churches against the backdrop of the Aegean Sea. Next, visit the village of Imerovigli, where you can take photos of the traditional buildings and winding streets. In the afternoon, take a sunset sail to the island of Thirassia, where you can take photos of the stunning sunsets over the Aegean Sea. End your day with a visit to the lighthouse in Akrotiri, where you can take photos of the stunning views of the island and the Aegean Sea.

Relaxation and Spa-Goer:
Start your day with a visit to one of the many thermal springs on the island, where you can relax and soak in the warm waters. Next, visit one of the many spa resorts on the island, where you can enjoy a massage or other spa treatments. In the afternoon, visit Perivolos Beach, where you can relax on the sand and soak up the sun. End your day with a relaxing dinner at a restaurant in Fira, where you can enjoy the views of the Aegean Sea as you sample some of the finest cuisines in Santorini.

Couples and Honeymooners:
Start your day with a romantic sunrise hike to the top of the ancient volcano, where you can enjoy breathtaking views of the island and the Aegean Sea. Next, take a private sail to the island of Thirassia, where you can enjoy a romantic picnic on the beach. In the afternoon, visit the village of Imerovigli, where you can take a romantic stroll through the winding streets and enjoy the views of the Aegean Sea. End your day with a romantic sunset dinner at a restaurant in Oia, where you can sample some of the finest cuisines in Santorini and enjoy the views of the Aegean Sea.

Adventure and Outdoors Enthusiast:
Start your day with a challenging hike up the ancient volcano, where you can enjoy stunning views of the island and the Aegean Sea. Next, visit Red Beach, where you can go snorkeling or swim in crystal-clear waters. In the afternoon, go windsurfing or kitesurfing at

Perissa Beach, where you can take advantage of the strong winds and waves. End your day with a sunset horseback ride along the beaches of the island, where you can enjoy the breathtaking views of the Aegean Sea as the sun sets.

Wine Lovers:
You can start your day with a visit to the Santo Wines winery, where you can take a tour and taste some of the finest wines produced on the island. Next, visit the Gavalas Vineyard, where you can learn about the traditional winemaking methods used on the island and taste some of the local wines. In the afternoon, visit the Estate Argyros Winery, where you can sample some of the rare and exclusive wines produced on the island. End your day with a wine-tasting dinner at a restaurant in Oia, where you can enjoy some of the finest cuisine in Santorini paired with local wines.

History and Archaeology Buffs:
Start your day with a visit to the ancient city of Akrotiri, where you can explore the ruins of one of the most well-preserved Minoan settlements. Next, visit the Archaeological Museum in Fira, where you can learn about the history and culture of the island. In the afternoon, visit the ancient Thira, where you can explore the ruins of the ancient city and learn about its rich history. End your day with a visit to the Prehistoric Thera Museum in Fira, where you can learn about the early history of the island and see some of the most important archaeological finds from the area.

Food and Drink

Traditional Cuisine of Santorini

From traditional dishes made with locally grown ingredients to innovative cuisine that combines local flavors with international influences, the cuisine of Santorini is a true delight for food lovers.

One of the standout features of Santorini's cuisine is its emphasis on fresh, locally-sourced ingredients. The fertile volcanic soil of the island produces some of the most delicious produce in Greece, including cherry tomatoes, fava beans, capers, and white eggplants. These ingredients are often used in traditional dishes like "domatokeftedes," which are fried tomato fritters, or "fava," a creamy yellow split pea puree.

Seafood is another staple of the Santorini diet, with the Aegean Sea providing a bountiful source of fish, octopus, squid, and other seafood. Fresh seafood is often grilled to perfection and served with a simple lemon and olive oil dressing, or used in traditional dishes like "calamari Santorini," which is a dish of fried squid served with a tangy tomato sauce.

Another hallmark of Santorini's cuisine is its wine, which is produced from grapes grown on the volcanic soil of the island. Santorini's wines are known for their distinct flavor, which is due to the unique climate and soil conditions of the island. Local wines like "Assyrtiko," "Vinsanto," and "Nykteri" are often enjoyed with meals and are a true reflection of the terroir of the island.

Santorini is also known for its sweets, which often incorporate ingredients like honey, almonds, and phyllo dough. "Loukoumades," which are deep-fried dough balls soaked in honey, and "amygdalota," which are almond cakes, are two of the most popular sweets on the island.

In addition to traditional cuisine, Santorini also offers a wide range of international dining options, from Italian to Mexican. However, it's the traditional dishes that truly capture the essence of the island, and offer a true taste of the Aegean.

Another important aspect of Santorini's cuisine is its use of herbs and spices, which add depth and complexity to the island's dishes. Fresh herbs like oregano, basil, and thyme are often used in traditional dishes like "moussaka," a layered eggplant and meat dish.

Additionally, local spices like cinnamon and cloves are used in sweets like "baklava," a flaky pastry made with phyllo dough, honey, and nuts.

Santorini is also known for its traditional dishes made with lamb, which is raised on the island. One of the most popular lamb dishes is "kleftiko," which is a slow-cooked lamb that is marinated in lemon and herbs and then baked in a clay oven. This dish is often served with roasted vegetables and potatoes and is a true reflection of the island's love of hearty, rustic fare.

For those with a sweet tooth, a visit to one of the many traditional patisseries on the island is a must. Here, you'll find a wide range of sweets and baked goods, from the aforementioned "loukoumades" and "amygdalota" to buttery croissants and delicate pastries. These sweets are the perfect way to enjoy a bit of indulgence after a long day of exploring the island.

In addition to traditional cuisine, Santorini also offers a thriving street food scene, with vendors selling everything from gyros and kebabs to fresh seafood and grilled meats. This is a great way to sample a variety of the island's dishes on the go and is a true reflection of the vibrant food culture that exists in Santorini.

Local Wine and Drinks

Santorini is a Greek island that is famous for its unique local wine, which is produced from grapes grown on the volcanic soil of the island. This soil, combined with the island's warm climate and harsh winds, creates a unique terroir that is reflected in the flavor of the wine.

One of the standout local wines is "Assyrtiko," a crisp, dry white wine that is known for its citrus and mineral flavors. This wine is made from the Assyrtiko grape, which is grown in vineyards on the southern part of the island. It is often enjoyed with seafood and other light dishes and is considered one of the best white wines produced in Greece.

Another popular local wine is "Vinsanto," a sweet dessert wine that is made from a blend of Assyrtiko, Aidani, and Athiri grapes. This wine is known for its rich, sweet flavor and is often enjoyed with desserts or as an after-dinner drink.

"Nykteri" is another local wine that is produced on the island, and is a dry white wine that is known for its floral and fruit flavors. This wine is made from the Athiri grape and is often enjoyed with lighter dishes like salads and seafood.

In addition to local wine, Santorini also has a thriving local spirits scene, with several traditional drinks that are made on the island. One of the most popular local drinks is "rakomelo," a warm drink made with raki, honey, and spices. This drink is often enjoyed during the colder months and is said to have medicinal properties.

Another popular local drink is "tsipouro," a clear spirit that is made from grapes and is similar to Italian grappa. This drink is often enjoyed as an aperitif or after dinner and is said to aid in digestion.

Santorini also has a thriving cocktail culture, with many bars and restaurants offering innovative drinks that incorporate local flavors and ingredients. From cocktails made with local wine and spirits to drinks made with fresh fruit and herbs, there's a drink for every taste and occasion.

Another important aspect of the local wine and drinks culture in Santorini is the annual Wine Festival, which takes place on the island every summer. During this festival, local wineries open their doors to visitors, offering tastings and tours of their vineyards and wineries. This is a great opportunity to sample a wide range of local wines and meet the winemakers and learn about their craft.

In addition to the Wine Festival, several wineries on the island offer year-round tastings and tours. These wineries range from small, family-run operations to larger commercial wineries, and offer visitors the chance to sample a variety of local wines and learn about the winemaking process.

For those who are interested in local spirits, several distilleries on the island offer tastings and tours. These distilleries produce a wide range of spirits, from raki and tsipouro to liqueurs made with local ingredients like honey, spices, and fruit.

Visitors to Santorini can also enjoy local drinks in a variety of settings, from traditional tavernas and cafes to stylish bars and nightclubs. Whether you prefer a quiet drink in a scenic spot or a night out on the town, there's a drink for every occasion in Santorini.

Best Restaurants and Tavernas

Santorini is famous for its delicious local cuisine, which combines traditional Greek flavors with the unique culinary influences of the Aegean. Whether you're looking for a gourmet dining experience or a casual taverna meal, there's a restaurant or taverna in Santorini to suit every taste and budget.

One of the best restaurants on the island is "Metropole," located in the charming village of Oia. This gourmet restaurant offers a sophisticated dining experience, with a menu that features creative dishes made with the freshest local ingredients. From fresh seafood to grilled meats and vegetables, the menu at Metropole is sure to impress.

Another top restaurant is "Niko's Taverna," located in the charming village of Fira. This traditional taverna serves up classic Greek dishes, made with the freshest local ingredients. Whether you're in the mood for moussaka, grilled meats, or fresh seafood, the menu at Niko's Taverna is sure to satisfy.

For a casual dining experience, there's "To Psaraki," a popular seafood taverna located in the fishing village of Ammoudi. This charming taverna serves up fresh, delicious seafood, caught daily from the Aegean. From grilled octopus and sardines to juicy shrimp and scallops, the menu at To Psaraki is sure to delight seafood lovers.

For those who are looking for a truly unique dining experience, there's "Sunset Fish Taverna," located in the village of Imerovigli. This popular taverna offers stunning views of the Aegean, along with a menu that features fresh seafood, grilled meats, and vegetables.

From the freshest local ingredients to the charming outdoor dining area, Sunset Fish Taverna is a must-visit for anyone looking for a memorable dining experience in Santorini.

Another great dining option in Santorini is "Avocado," located in the village of Perissa. This stylish restaurant offers a menu that features creative Mediterranean cuisine, made with the freshest local ingredients.

Whether you're in the mood for grilled octopus, roasted vegetables, or hand-made pasta, the menu at Avocado is sure to impress. For those who are looking for a more casual dining experience, there's "Kapari Wine Restaurant," located in the village of Imerovigli.

This charming taverna serves up traditional Greek dishes, made with the freshest local ingredients and paired with some of the island's best local wines. From juicy grilled meats to fresh seafood, the menu at Kapari Wine Restaurant is sure to satisfy.

For a true taste of traditional Santorinian cuisine, there's "Ta Karamanlidika Tou Fani," located in the village of Fira. This popular taverna serves up classic dishes, made with ingredients sourced from the island's lush gardens and farms.

From stuffed tomatoes and peppers to moussaka and pastitsio, the menu at Ta Karamanlidika Tou Fani is a true reflection of Santorinian culinary traditions.

If you're looking for a more upscale dining experience, there's "Santo Wines Restaurant," located in the village of Pyrgos. This sophisticated restaurant offers a menu that features gourmet dishes, made with the freshest local ingredients and paired with some of the best local wines.

From grilled meats and vegetables to fresh seafood and pasta, the menu at Santo Wines Restaurant is sure to impress.

Beaches and Outdoor Activities

Types of Beaches

Santorini is a popular Greek island known for its stunning beaches and crystal-clear waters. The island offers a variety of beaches that cater to different tastes and preferences, ranging from busy and lively to secluded and peaceful. Here are some of the most popular types of beaches in Santorini:

- **Black Sand Beaches**: Santorini is famous for its black sand beaches, which are created by the volcanic activity on the island. Some of the most popular black sand beaches include Perissa, Kamari, and Monolithos. These beaches offer a unique experience, with the dark sand contrasting against the bright blue waters.

- **Red Sand Beaches**: Another unique type of beach in Santorini is the red sand beach. As the name suggests, these beaches have red sand, which is also a result of volcanic activity. The most popular red sand beach in Santorini is Red Beach.

- **White Sand Beaches**: If you're looking for a more traditional beach experience, you can also find white sand beaches in Santorini. Some of the most popular white sand beaches include Vlychada, Baxedes, and Paradise Beach. These beaches offer a more traditional beach atmosphere and are perfect for swimming and sunbathing.

- **Cliff-side Beaches**: Santorini's dramatic cliff-side geography also offers a unique type of beach experience. Beaches like Amoudi Bay and Armeni

Beach are accessible only by steps cut into the cliffs and offer breathtaking views of the Aegean Sea.

- **Secluded Beaches**: If you're looking for a more intimate and secluded beach experience, you can find hidden coves and secluded beaches around Santorini. Some of the most popular secluded beaches include Eros Beach, Almyra Beach, and Koloumbos Beach.

Recommended Beaches and Activities

- **Perissa Beach**: Perissa is one of the most popular black sand beaches in Santorini and is perfect for those who love a lively atmosphere. You can lounge on the beach, swim in the clear waters, or enjoy a variety of water sports like jet-skiing and parasailing. There are also several bars and restaurants along the beach where you can grab a bite to eat or enjoy a drink.

- **Kamari Beach**: Kamari is another popular black sand beach in Santorini and offers a similar atmosphere to Perissa. Along with swimming and sunbathing, you can also rent sun loungers, umbrellas, and water sports equipment. There are also several bars and restaurants in the area, as well as shops for souvenirs and gifts.

- **Red Beach**: The Red Beach is a must-visit for those who love to explore unique and unusual destinations. The beach is a stunning shade of red, due to the surrounding cliffs, and is perfect for swimming and sunbathing. You can also hike along the cliff-side trails for stunning views of the Aegean Sea.

- **Vlychada Beach**: Vlychada is a peaceful and serene white sand beach, perfect for those who want to escape the busy crowds. The beach is surrounded by cliffs and is a great place for snorkeling and exploring the local marine life. There are also several restaurants and cafes nearby, serving traditional Greek cuisine.

- **Amoudi Bay**: Amoudi Bay is a stunning cliff-side beach that is only accessible by steps cut into the cliffs. The bay offers breathtaking views of the Aegean Sea and is perfect for swimming and sunbathing. You can also enjoy fresh seafood at one of the local tavernas and take a scenic boat tour of the surrounding coastline.

- **Baxedes Beach**: Baxedes is a secluded white sand beach that is perfect for those who want to escape the busy crowds. The beach is surrounded by cliffs and is ideal for swimming, sunbathing, and snorkeling. There are also several restaurants and cafes in the area, serving traditional Greek cuisine.

- **Monolithos Beach**: Monolithos is a black sand beach that is known for its clear waters and stunning views of the Aegean Sea. The beach is perfect for swimming and sunbathing, and is also a great spot for families, with shallow waters and calm surf. There are also several restaurants and bars in the area, serving traditional Greek food and drinks.

- **Armeni Beach**: Armeni Beach is a stunning cliff-side beach that is only accessible by steps cut into the cliffs. The beach offers breathtaking views of the Aegean Sea and is perfect for swimming, sunbathing, and snorkeling. There are also several restaurants and cafes nearby, serving fresh seafood and traditional Greek dishes.

- **Paradise Beach**: Paradise Beach is a popular white sand beach that is known for its lively atmosphere and stunning views. The beach is perfect for swimming, sunbathing, and participating in water sports like jet-skiing and parasailing. There are also several bars and restaurants in the area, serving drinks and delicious food.

- **Eros Beach**: Eros Beach is a secluded white sand beach that is perfect for those who want to escape the busy crowds. The beach is surrounded by cliffs and is ideal for swimming, sunbathing, and snorkeling. There are also several restaurants and cafes in the area, serving traditional Greek cuisine.

Water Sports and Excursions

- **Scuba Diving**: Santorini's crystal-clear waters offer excellent visibility for scuba diving. The island's underwater world is full of vibrant marine life and ancient ruins. Divers can explore the famous volcanic hot springs, underwater caves, and shipwrecks. Several dive centers on the island offer guided dives and equipment rentals.

- **Snorkeling**: For those who prefer to stay afloat, snorkeling is a great way to explore Santorini's underwater world. The waters around the island are teeming with colorful fish, octopuses, and other marine life. There are several snorkeling excursions available that take visitors to the best spots around the island.

- **Kayaking**: Santorini's dramatic coastline, hidden coves, and turquoise waters make it a great destination for kayaking. Paddle along the coast and take in the views of the iconic white-washed buildings and volcanic cliffs. Kayaking is a great way to explore the island's secluded beaches and get up close and personal with the local marine life.

- **Yacht Tours**: For a more luxurious way to experience the island, consider a yacht tour. Several companies offer private and group yacht tours around Santorini. These tours often include stops at secluded beaches, snorkeling and diving spots, and breathtaking views of the island's famous sunset.

- **Parasailing**: For an unforgettable experience, try parasailing over

Santorini's stunning coastline. Soar high above the crystal-clear waters and take in the breathtaking views of the island's unique architecture and dramatic coastline.

- **Windsurfing**: Santorini is a great destination for windsurfing, with its consistent winds and open waters. Several windsurfing schools on the island offer lessons and equipment rentals for all skill levels. Whether you're a beginner or an experienced windsurfer, you'll find the perfect conditions for this exciting sport in Santorini.

- **Stand-Up Paddleboarding (SUP)**: Stand-Up Paddleboarding is a fun and relaxing way to explore Santorini's waterways. Glide over the calm waters, taking in the views of the island's stunning coastline and white-washed buildings. SUP is a great activity for families and groups, as it's easy to learn and suitable for all ages.

- **Beach Hopping**: Santorini has some of the most beautiful beaches in Greece, and what better way to enjoy them than by taking a beach hopping tour. These tours typically take visitors to some of the island's most famous and secluded beaches, including Red Beach, White Beach, and Perissa Beach.

- **Boat Rentals**: For a more self-guided excursion, consider renting a boat and exploring the island on your own. Several boat rental companies on the island offer different sizes and types of boats, from small inflatables to large motorboats. With a rented boat, you can set your own pace and see the sights that interest you the most.

- **Fishing Tours**: For a unique experience, try a fishing tour in Santorini. These tours typically take visitors out to the open waters around the island where they can try their hand at fishing for a variety of species, including mackerel, grouper, and sea bream. Fishing tours are a great way to experience the local culture and traditions while enjoying a day on the water.

Nightlife and Shopping

Bars, Clubs, and Nightlife

Bars:

- **Enigma Lounge Bar**: This stylish bar located in the heart of the island's capital, Fira, is the perfect place to enjoy a cocktail or two as you watch the sunset. With its comfortable seating, amazing views, and a menu of creative cocktails, Enigma is a must-visit for anyone looking for a fun and relaxed bar experience.

- **Lava Cocktail Bar**: Located in the village of Imerovigli, this bar offers an incredible view of the Aegean Sea. The bar is known for its stunning sunsets, delicious cocktails, and lively atmosphere. Whether you're looking to relax with a drink or meet new people, Lava Cocktail Bar is a great choice.

Clubs:

- **Babylon Club**: This club is the biggest and most popular nightlife spot in Santorini. With a large dance floor, state-of-the-art sound system, and talented DJs, it's the perfect place to party until the early hours of the morning. Whether you're into techno, house, or pop, Babylon Club is sure to have something to suit your taste.

Space Club: This open-air club offers breathtaking views of the Aegean Sea and is one of the most popular spots for young people in Santorini. With a lively atmosphere, top-notch DJs, and plenty of room to dance, Space Club is a great place to let loose and have a good time.

Nightlife:

- **Fira**: The capital of Santorini is known for its lively nightlife, with a wide range of bars, clubs, and tavernas to choose from. Whether you're looking to enjoy a drink and watch the sunset or dance the night away, Fira has something to offer everyone.

- **Oia**: This picturesque village is known for its stunning sunsets and tranquil atmosphere, but it also has a vibrant nightlife scene. With a range of bars and tavernas that stay open late, Oia is the perfect place to enjoy a drink and relax after a day of exploring the island.

One of the great things about the nightlife in Santorini is the variety of options available. From trendy bars and clubs to more laid-back tavernas and wine bars, there's something to suit every taste and preference. If you're looking to enjoy a relaxing drink, there are plenty of spots that offer stunning views of the Aegean Sea, as well as a menu of creative cocktails, fine wine, and traditional Greek spirits.

For those looking to party, there are plenty of clubs and bars to choose from, with top-notch DJs and lively crowds that keep the party going until the early hours of the morning. Whether you're into techno, house, or pop, there's sure to be a club that caters to your musical tastes.

One of the best things about the nightlife in Santorini is the stunning scenery and breathtaking views that can be enjoyed from many of the bars and clubs. From the dramatic cliffs of Oia to the bustling streets of Fira, there's a spot for everyone to enjoy the island's beauty by night.

Shopping in Santorini

One of the most popular shopping areas on the island is the capital city of Thira, where you'll find a variety of stores selling everything from jewelry and clothing to handmade ceramics and local crafts. Some of the most popular items to purchase as souvenirs from Santorini include handmade pottery, Greek olive oil and wine, and local spices.

If you're looking for high-end fashion, you can find designer boutiques in Thira and Oia. These stores offer a wide selection of designer clothing, shoes, and accessories from top brands such as Gucci, Prada, and Chanel.

Santorini is also known for its unique jewelry shops, which feature traditional Greek designs made from gold and silver. Many of these shops offer customized jewelry services, allowing you to create a unique piece that is specific to your style.

For those interested in traditional Greek arts and crafts, the island's many art galleries offer a diverse selection of paintings, sculptures, and ceramics made by local artists. These galleries are a great place to pick up a one-of-a-kind piece to take home with you.

Finally, if you're looking for a more authentic shopping experience, be sure to visit the local markets in Santorini. These markets offer a wide variety of goods, including fresh produce, clothing, and handmade goods. You can also find local vendors selling traditional Greek foods and spices, making it a great place to pick up some ingredients for a home-cooked meal.

Local Products and Souvenirs

Santorini is a treasure trove of local products and souvenirs that offer a glimpse into the island's rich history and culture. Whether you're looking for traditional Greek items or unique gifts to bring back home, there are plenty of options to choose from.

One of the most popular local products in Santorini is its renowned wine. The volcanic soil and mild climate of the island make it perfect for growing grapes, and Santorini produces some of the finest wines in Greece. Visitors can visit local wineries to sample the various types of wine, including the famous Vinsanto dessert wine.

Another popular local product in Santorini is its delicious olive oil. The island is famous for its high-quality olive oil, which is produced from local olive groves. Olive oil is used in many traditional Greek dishes and is a popular souvenir item among visitors.

Handmade pottery is another popular local product in Santorini. The island is renowned for its traditional pottery techniques, and visitors can find a variety of ceramics, plates, and bowls in local shops and markets. These items make excellent gifts and souvenirs, and many visitors choose to purchase handmade pieces to bring back home.

For those interested in traditional Greek arts and crafts, Santorini offers a wide selection of items, including woven textiles, wooden sculptures, and paintings. These items are often handmade by local artists and provide a unique glimpse into the island's cultural heritage.

Finally, if you're looking for unique souvenirs, consider picking up some local spices, such as thyme, oregano, and rosemary, or a bottle of traditional Greek liqueur, such as ouzo or tsipouro. These items offer a taste of Greece and make excellent gifts for friends and family back home.

CONCLUSION

Santorini is truly a gem in the Aegean Sea that should not be missed. From the breathtaking sunsets and stunning caldera views to the picturesque villages and ancient ruins, this island offers a unique and unforgettable experience.

The crystal-clear waters, gorgeous beaches, and vibrant nightlife make it an ideal destination for those seeking adventure and relaxation. However, this island is not only beautiful on the outside. Santorini's rich history and cultural heritage offer a fascinating glimpse into the past and a chance to immerse yourself in the local way of life.

Whether you're a history buff, a foodie, or simply looking for a stunning place to unwind, Santorini has something to offer. So, take a deep breath, soak up the stunning views, and revel in the beauty of this Greek island paradise. Your time in Santorini will be a memory you will cherish for a lifetime.

Printed in Great Britain
by Amazon